Countries of the World

Argentina

by Muriel L. Dubois

Bridgestone Books
an imprint of Capstone Press
Mankato, Minnesota

Bridgestone Books are published by Capstone Press
151 Good Counsel Drive, P.O. Box 669, Mankato, Minnesota 56002
http://www.capstone-press.com

Library of Congress Cataloging-in-Publication Data
Dubois, Muriel L.
    Argentina/by Muriel L. Dubois.
    p. cm.—(Countries of the world)
    Includes bibliographical references and index.
    ISBN 0-7368-0811-6
    1. Argentina—Juvenile literature. I. Title. II. Countries of the world (Mankato, Minn.)
F2808.2 .D83 2001
982—dc21   00-009788

Summary: Discusses the landscape, culture, food, animals, sports, and holidays of Argentina.

Editorial Credits
Erika Mikkelson, editor; Karen Risch, product planning editor; Linda Clavel, production designer
    and illustrator; Katy Kudela, photo researcher

Photo Credits
Joe Viesti/The Viesti Collection, Inc., 20
TRIP/ASK Images, cover
Victor Englebert, 6, 8, 10, 12
Visuals Unlimited/Erwin C. Nielsen, 14; Milton H. Tierney, Jr., 16; Francis/Donna Caldwell, 18

**Bridgestone Books would like to thank John Rattagan, researcher at Guinness World
    Records, for his help in reviewing this text.**

1 2 3 4 5 6 06 05 04 03 02 01

Table of Contents

Fast Facts

Name: Argentine Republic
Capital: Buenos Aires
Population: Nearly 37 million
Language: Spanish
Religion: Roman Catholic

Size: 1,068,296 square miles
(2,766,890 square kilometers)
*Argentina is twice as big as the U.S.
state of Alaska.*
Crops: Corn, wheat, soybeans

Maps

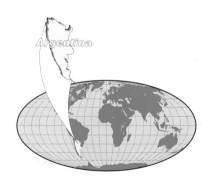

Flag

The Argentine flag has three horizontal stripes. The outer stripes are light blue. The middle stripe is white. The blue stripes stand for the color of Argentina's sky. A golden sun with a human face is in the center of the flag. It is called the Sun of May. This symbol honors the Revolution of 1810. Buenos Aires became free from Spain on May 25, 1810.

Currency

The unit of currency in Argentina is the peso. One hundred centavos make up one peso.

In 2000, one peso was equal to about one U.S. dollar. About 70 centavos equaled one Canadian dollar.

The Land

Argentina is in southeastern South America. The Atlantic Ocean borders Argentina on the east and south. The Andes Mountains divide Argentina from Chile on the west. Bolivia and Paraguay border Argentina to the north. Brazil and Uruguay lie to the northeast.

Argentina has different types of land. Mesopotamia is a rich farming region in the northeast. Argentina's two largest rivers, the Río de la Plata and the Paraná, flow through this area. The Gran Chaco is an area with thick forests. The Gran Chaco and Mesopotamia receive a great deal of rain.

The Pampas is in the center of Argentina. Farmers raise Argentina's famous beef cattle on this flat grassland. Patagonia is in the south. Small trees and cactuses grow in this desert area. Farmers must bring in water for crops. Patagonia is a good place to raise sheep.

Rivers flow through Patagonia's dry land.

Life at Home

More than two-thirds of the people in Argentina live in cities. Buenos Aires has many barrios or neighborhoods. La Boca is a colorful artists' neighborhood. The city's poorest people live in villa miserias. These areas of crowded, run-down shacks have no heat or water.

Some Argentine families live in the country. Wealthy people own large ranches there. Their homes look European. Some people own small farm houses. The very poor might live in small mud huts.

Argentine families are close. They are loyal to each other. Many family members might share one home. Grandparents, aunts, or uncles sometimes live with the family. Each child also has godparents. Children call their godmother madrina (mah-DREE-nah). They call their godfather padrino (pah-DREE-noh). Godparents act as a child's second parents.

Time together as a family is important to Argentines.

Going to School

Public school is free for all Argentine children. The Argentine school year lasts from March to December. Children go to school from 8:00 to 12:00 in the morning or 1:00 to 5:00 in the afternoon.

Students spend eight years in primary school. They learn reading, math, social studies, science, and art. Children also study English, French, and Italian. All primary school students wear a uniform. Children at public schools wear a long, white top called a guardapolvo.

After primary school, children attend secondary school. Children study many subjects for two years. Their studies may include geography, chemistry, or history. During the last two years, students pick special subjects. These subjects prepare students for work or college.

Education is important in Argentina. Nearly all Argentines can read and write.

Argentine Food

Some favorite Argentine foods come from their European ancestors. Italian foods such as lasagna, ravioli, and spaghetti are especially popular in Argentina.

Argentines eat gnocchi (NAW-kee). These small rolls are made from boiled potato dough. Cooks serve gnocchi with a tomato sauce made with beef called tuco (TOO-koh).

Argentines eat beef at nearly every meal. Asado is barbecued beef. Espanadas are pastries shaped like half-moons. Espanadas are filled with spices, beef, olives, and raisins.

The most popular drink in Argentina is yerba maté (ZHER-bah MAH-tay). This herbal tea comes from a small evergreen tree. Hot water is poured over its leaves. Argentines drink the tea from a small round cup or gourd. They sip the tea through a straw that filters out the tea leaves.

Many Argentines eat a thick corn stew called locro.

Gauchos

In the 1700s, many horses and cattle ran wild on the Pampas. Rich landowners hired gauchos to train the horses. These Argentine cowboys used the horses to herd the cattle.

Gauchos loved life on the Pampas. They were independent, hardworking, and brave. Gauchos are one of Argentina's symbols. Stories, poems, and songs tell about gauchos.

The word gaucho may come from a native word, huacho. Huacho means orphan. The gaucho lived without a family while he worked.

Gauchos wore loose pants tucked inside riding boots. A woolen cape called a poncho kept gauchos warm. Guachos wore a brimmed hat that kept the sun out of their eyes. Today, gauchos perform in rodeos. People dress like gauchos during special holidays. Some gauchos still herd cattle on Argentina's Pampas.

Some gauchos perform in rodeos.

Animals

Four members of the camel family live in Argentina's Andes Mountains. Farmers raise llamas and alpacas for their wool. Guanacos and vicuñas are smaller animals from the camel family.

The forests of Argentina are home to several animals. Jaguars, howler monkeys, tapirs, and coatí live in the forests. Tapirs are about the size of hogs. They are plant-eaters related to the rhinoceros and the horse. The coatí is a member of the raccoon family. It has a long, narrow face.

The carpincho lives near the Paraná River. It is the world's largest rodent. A carpincho can weigh more than 100 pounds (45 kilograms).

The cavy lives in Patagonia. This animal is a long-eared guinea pig. It digs holes in the ground.

The southern tip of Patagonia is near the Antarctic Circle. Penguins, elephant seals, and sea lions live on the southern coast.

The coatí is about the same size as a raccoon.

Sports

Many of Argentina's sports come from Europe. Soccer is the most popular sport in Argentina. It is called fútbol (FOOT-ball). Argentina won the World Cup in 1978 and 1986. Teams from around the world compete in this soccer tournament.

Argentines enjoy many other sports. Many play tennis. Car racing, boxing, and rugby also are popular.

Gauchos played pato (PAH-toh). Pato means duck. Gauchos once used a real duck in this sport. Today, riders try to move a ball toward a goal with their hands. The ball is made of leather and has six handles. The rider must reach down from his horse to grab the pato.

Many Argentines enjoy mountain climbing. People from all over the world come to climb Mount Aconcagua. It is the highest peak in the Western Hemisphere.

The British brought soccer to Argentina in the 1800s.

Holidays and Celebrations

Argentines celebrate two Independence Days. On May 25, they remember when Buenos Aires became free from Spain in 1810. Six years later, on July 9, all of Argentina became free. People throughout Argentina celebrate both days.

Many holidays are based on Catholic holy days. Argentines celebrate Carnival six weeks before Easter. People go to dances and parties. On Christmas Eve, families gather together. They eat special foods and sometimes dance. They watch fireworks at midnight.

September 21 is Students' Day. Children and their teachers get together for picnics and games on Students' Day. This date also is the first day of spring in Argentina. Because the earth is tilted, Argentina experiences spring when it is fall in the United States.

Some people dress in costumes during Carnival.

Hands On: Play Rayuela

Rayuela (rah-shoo-AH-lah) is the Argentine name for hopscotch.

What You Need

Sidewalk chalk

A small stone for each player

Driveway, sidewalk, or cement area

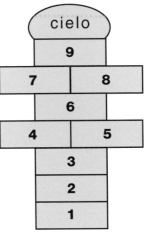

What You Do

1. Draw a rayuela playing field on the ground like the diagram to the right.

2. The object of the game is to hop on one foot from boxes 1 to cielo and back ten times. When two boxes are side by side, players should land with one foot in each box.

3. On each turn a player throws a stone in one box and hops over that box. Players first throw the stone in box 1, then box 2, and so on. On the way back down the playing field the player picks up the stone before hopping in the box.

4. Players lose their turn if they hop in a box with a stone in it. Players also lose their turn if they step on a line or throw a stone outside of a box.

5. Players continue taking turns. On each turn players begin on the number they missed. The winner is the first person to land their stone in "cielo." Cielo means heaven in Spanish. The player must hop back down the playing field to win.

Learn to Speak Spanish

yes	sí	(SEE)
no	no	(NOH)
hello	hola	(OH-lah)
good-bye	chau	(CHOW)
mother	madre	(MAH-dray)
father	padre	(PAH-dray)

Words to Know

ancestor (AN-sess-tur)—a person from whom one is descended, such as a great-grandfather

barrio (BA-ree-oh)—a neighborhood in a large city

godparent (GOD-pair-uhnt)—someone who promises his or her support for a child when the child is baptized into the Christian religion

gourd (GORD)—a fruit whose hard, dry shell is used for cups and bowls

herbal (URB-uhl)—made from plants that are used for cooking

orphan (OR-fuhn)—a child whose parents have died

rugby (RUHG-bee)—a form of football played by two teams that kick, pass, or carry an oval ball

Read More

Burgan, Michael. *Argentina.* A True Book. New York: Children's Press, 1999.

Frank, Nicole. *Argentina.* Countries of the World. Milwaukee: Gareth Stevens, 2000.

Useful Addresses and Internet Sites

Argentine Tourist Information Office
12 West 56th Street
New York, NY 10019

Embassy of the Argentine Republic
90 Sparks Street Suite 910
Ottawa, ON K1P 5B4
Canada

República Argentina—Secretaría de Turismo
http://www.wam.com.ar/tourism/g/reg6/reg6.htm
The World Factbook 2000—Argentina
http://www.odci.gov/cia/publications/factbook/geos/ar.html

Index